LITTLE LIBRARY

Helicopters

Christopher Maynard

Kingfisher Books

NEW YORK

Contents

Landing sites

Helicopters have one big advantage over airplanes, or fixed-wing planes. They can go almost anywhere. All they need to take off or land is a small patch of flat ground. It could be the corner of an airport, the top of a skyscraper, or the side of a mountain.

That's why helicopters are so often used as air taxis, and for carrying out rescue missions in remote places.

Inside a helicopter

All helicopters have a cockpit in the front where the crew sit. Some helicopters have only one engine, while others have two or even three.

Instead of fixed wings, a helicopter has spinning blades called rotors. Usually, there is a main rotor near the front that lifts the helicopter up, and a small one at the back for steering.

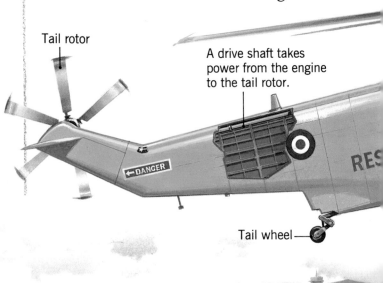

Tail rotor

A drive shaft takes power from the engine to the tail rotor.

←DANGER

RES

Tail wheel

Helicopters are sometimes known as choppers or egg-beaters, because of the chopping sound of their rotors as they whip through the air.

The chopper below is a Sea King. It has two engines, a big main rotor and a smaller tail rotor.

Winch for rescuing people

Gearbox

One of two engines

Main rotor

Cockpit

RESCUE

A float on each side keeps the helicopter level if it lands on water.

Cargo deck for carrying heavy loads

Main wheel

Into the air

A helicopter is kept in the air by its spinning main rotor. As the blades turn, they produce an upward pull called lift. The faster the rotor turns, the greater the lift.

When the strength of lift is more than the weight of the helicopter, it makes the machine rise into the air.

Fixed-wing planes create lift by moving forward. That's why they race down runways to take off.

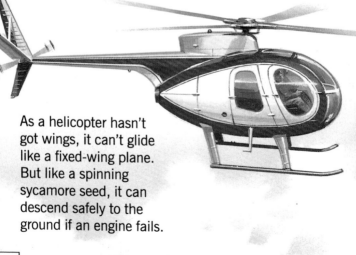

As a helicopter hasn't got wings, it can't glide like a fixed-wing plane. But like a spinning sycamore seed, it can descend safely to the ground if an engine fails.

CREATING LIFT

The main rotor cannot raise a helicopter off the ground just by spinning around fast. As long as the blades of the rotor are set to a flat position, they will not produce any lift.

As the angle of the rotor blades is increased, they start to dig into the air instead of slicing through it. This creates the lift that makes the helicopter rise into the air.

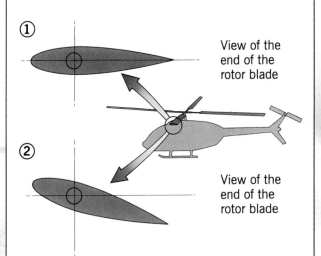

① View of the end of the rotor blade

② View of the end of the rotor blade

1 A rotor blade set at a flat angle just spins round and round and creates no lift at all.

2 When the rotor blade is slightly angled, it digs into the air, lifting the helicopter.

Rotors

There are three basic rotor layouts. One has a main rotor on top and a small rotor at the tail. Another has a main rotor both at the front and the back. The third is less common and has two main rotors on top of each other.

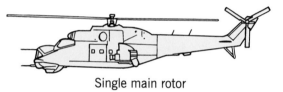

Single main rotor

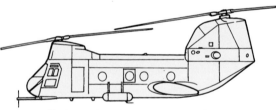

Twin main rotors, one at each end

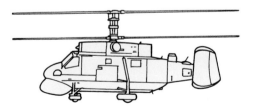

Twin rotors, one above the other

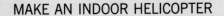

MAKE AN INDOOR HELICOPTER

You will need a pencil and some cardboard.
1 Cut a strip of cardboard 8 inches x 1 inch.
2 Make a small hole in the center. Cut out the two triangular slots.

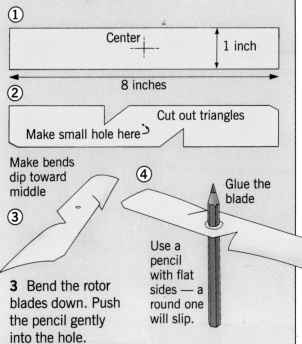

①

Center | 1 inch

8 inches

②

Make small hole here ⤸   Cut out triangles

Make bends dip toward middle

③

Glue the blade

Use a pencil with flat sides — a round one will slip.

3 Bend the rotor blades down. Push the pencil gently into the hole.
4 Use glue or some adhesive putty to attach the pencil to the wing.
5 Hold the bottom of the pencil in your fingertips. Flick the pencil to make it spin into the air. Watch your helicopter rise as the rotating blades create lift.

④

The controls

A helicopter can fly in any direction. It can fly up and down, forward, sideways and even backward.

There are three main helicopter controls. These are the rudder pedals, the cyclic pitch control, and the collective pitch control. The collective pitch control changes the angle of the rotor blades to alter the amount of lift.

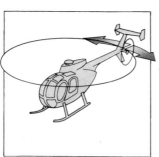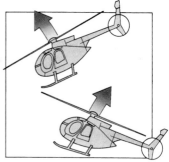

The rudder pedals control the tail rotor to keep the helicopter pointed in the exact direction the pilot wishes to go. It is used like the rudder on a boat or plane.

The cyclic pitch control tilts, or pitches, the main rotor to make the helicopter fly in different directions. For example, if the main rotor is tilted forward, the helicopter will fly straight ahead.

IN THE COCKPIT

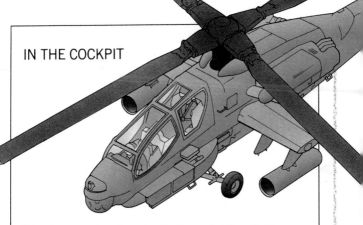

The two-seater Apache is flown by the U.S. Army. It is used to attack enemy tanks, and carries guns, rockets, and missiles. The pilot sits behind the gunner in a raised rear seat. The gunner is in charge of the aiming and firing equipment.

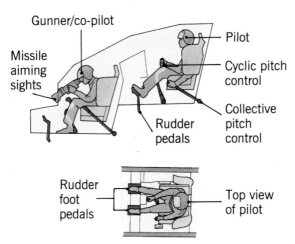

Gunner/co-pilot

Pilot

Missile aiming sights

Cyclic pitch control

Rudder pedals

Collective pitch control

Rudder foot pedals

Top view of pilot

13

Taking off

T o take off, the pilot operates the
   collective pitch control to angle
the rotor blades. The steeper the angle,
the greater the lift. A control called the
throttle is used to increase the engine
power, making the main rotor whirl so
fast that the blades cannot be seen.

As the helicopter climbs into the air,
the pilot tilts the main rotor unit
forward and the helicopter
is on its way.

A Gazelle can travel
for 500 miles
(800 km) on a full
tank of fuel. Its top
speed is 163 mph
(262 km/h).

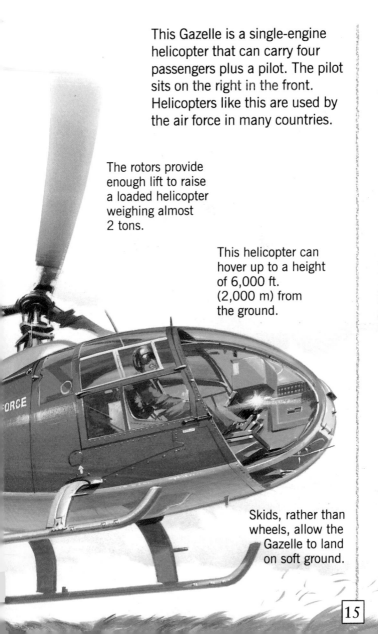

This Gazelle is a single-engine helicopter that can carry four passengers plus a pilot. The pilot sits on the right in the front. Helicopters like this are used by the air force in many countries.

The rotors provide enough lift to raise a loaded helicopter weighing almost 2 tons.

This helicopter can hover up to a height of 6,000 ft. (2,000 m) from the ground.

Skids, rather than wheels, allow the Gazelle to land on soft ground.

At work

H elicopters are made in all sizes. Small machines are often used as air taxis. Bigger machines carry cargo or passengers over longer distances, such as ferrying people and equipment to and from oil rigs at sea.

▽ The Alouette III is used by the police.

▽ The Sikorsky S-55 is used by the military and the building industry.

◁ This BO 105 can be used as an ambulance.

▽ A Boeing 243 can carry over 40 people.

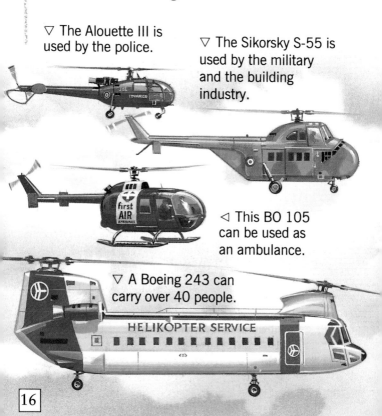

HELIKOPTER SERVICE

SHAKEN BY NOISE

During a flight, the spinning rotors and the noise of the roaring engine can shake bits of machinery loose, such as nuts and bolts. That's why engineers have to check helicopter engines very carefully after every flight.

Try this experiment and discover just how powerful these sound vibrations can be.

1 Stretch a piece of plastic wrap over the top of an empty jar. Put a rubber band around the top to keep it tight.

2 Sprinkle a little sugar on the top.
3 Hold an empty tin near the jar and bang it with a wooden spoon. The sugar will bounce around. This is caused by the noise vibrations coming from the tin.

The heliport

A base for helicopters is called a heliport. It does the same job as an airport, but takes up a much smaller amount of space.

A big circled "H" marks the place where helicopters land and take off. Then, when they need to be repaired, they are wheeled into a large hangar.

KEY TO THE HELIPORT

① Helicopters lift off into the air.

② The "H" marks the landing site.

③ The hangar is used to service the helicopters.

④ Between flights, engineers check the helicopter.

⑤ Tools and spares are stored in the hangar.

⑥ A windsock shows which way the wind is blowing.

⑦ A fire crew waits for an emergency.

⑧ Passengers check in at the terminal.

Rescue at sea

Because helicopters can hover in one spot and lift someone to safety, they are often used to rescue people from the sea.

The busiest air-sea rescue station is at Miami, Florida, where they fly about 800 rescue missions a year.

1 A typical story of a rescue begins with an accident at sea. Some time later the empty boat is spotted and the coastguard is alerted by radio.

2 A Dolphin helicopter takes off and goes to the area where the empty boat was last seen. Flying low, the crew search the area.

3 Luckily the missing sailor is still alive. He is able to haul himself into the rescue cage that has been lowered to him on the end of a strong steel cable.

Helicopters at war

Helicopters are often used by armies and air forces. The larger helicopters carry weapons and soldiers. Others often serve as air ambulances and take the wounded to hospital.

Special attack helicopters can hunt and destroy tanks with rockets. While others carry fast-firing guns to use against enemy troops on the ground.

Some types of military helicopter have a periscope sight above the main rotor. The pilot takes aim while the helicopter is hidden, then flies up to fire the missile.

A MODEL PERISCOPE

This is a periscope you can use to see over walls and around corners. But don't make it too long or it will flop around.

You'll need a sheet of stiff cardboard and two small mirrors exactly the same size.

1 Draw the pattern onto the cardboard and cut it out. Also cut out the rectangle at the top.

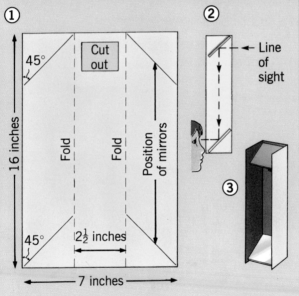

2 Fold the cardboard along the dotted lines.
3 Now glue the angled mirrors to the top and bottom. Check that the reflecting sides of the mirrors are facing each other.

On patrol

Because helicopters can fly slowly
and hover, they can do lots of jobs
that other aircraft can't do. They can
lift and carry heavy loads, or quickly
check on traffic jams. Sometimes the
police use them to patrol cities at night.
If a helicopter is fitted with a search-
light, it can light up even the darkest
alley to see what's going on.

△ A flying crane, like
this Chinook, can lift a
12-ton load.

▷ The police in this Bell
helicopter use a search-
light to track a criminal.

Heliplanes

The Osprey is half-helicopter, half-plane. It has tilting rotors at the ends of its wings. The rotors work just like the main rotor on a helicopter when the Osprey is taking off. But then they swing down and work like the propellers on a fixed-wing plane.

HELICOPTER DISGUISES

Forests

Deserts

Seas

Military helicopters are painted in camouflage colors so they blend with their background.

A helicopter fleet

M any different helicopters fly with the world's airlines and armed forces. They have more uses than any other kind of aircraft.

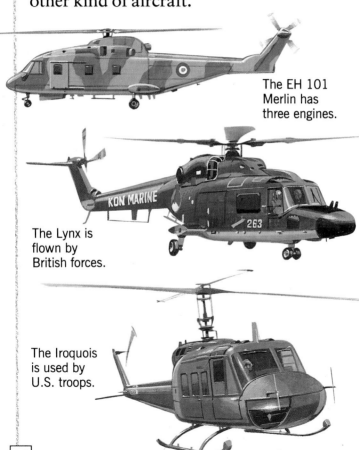

The EH 101 Merlin has three engines.

The Lynx is flown by British forces.

The Iroquois is used by U.S. troops.

The Seahawk
is flown by
the U.S. Navy.

The Robinson R22
is cheap and easy
to fly. It is used
for training.

The Dauphin
is a fast,
French-made
helicopter.

The BK 117 is a
German-Japanese
machine.

Index